# ONE
# UNO

## One-Handed Non-Traditional Expression for Patients who had a Stroke

Uso de una mano de forma No tradicional para obtener mejor
expresion en pacientes con infarto cerebral (derrame)

# ROBERTO G. MIXCO

WESTBOW·
PRESS
A DIVISION OF THOMAS NELSON
& ZONDERVAN

WestBow Press books may be ordered through booksellers or by contacting:

WestBow Press
A Division of Thomas Nelson & Zondervan
1663 Liberty Drive
Bloomington, IN 47403
www.westbowpress.com
1 (866) 928-1240

Because of the dynamic nature of the Internet, any web addresses or
links contained in this book may have changed since publication and may
no longer be valid. The views expressed in this work are solely those
of the author and do not necessarily reflect the views of the publisher,
and the publisher hereby disclaims any responsibility for them.

Any people depicted in stock imagery provided by Thinkstock are models,
and such images are being used for illustrative purposes only.
Certain stock imagery © Thinkstock.

ISBN: 978-1-4908-5744-2 (sc)
ISBN: 978-1-4908-5743-5 (hc)

Library of Congress Control Number: 2014920471

Printed in the United States of America.

WestBow Press rev. date: 12/11/2014

# O N E

One-handed
Non traditional
Expression for patients
who have had
a stroke

# UNO

Uso de una mano de forma

No tradicional para

Obtener mejor expresión en
pacientes con infarto
cerebral (derrame)

# Contents

# Indice

# Introduction

Various conditions can affect people's ability to communicate, such as head trauma, brain tumors, pathology at the vocal cords, hearing loss, and stroke, to name a few. However, for our purposes, we will focus on stroke, an illness common in the United States and all over the world. As a neurologist of more than twenty five years, I have seen the aggravation that patients and their families experience when someone suffers a stroke. Many people affected by stroke lose their ability to communicate; at times, the patient is unable to speak at all, and at other times the families or caretakers cannot understand the patient. This inability to communicate frustrates the patient and can eventually lead him or her into depression. For loved ones, friends, and caretakers to better converse with and care for the individual, they must understand the different ways in which patients may be affected. Here are the three most common:

- inability to express oneself, or expressive aphasia
- inability to understand others, or receptive aphasia
- various combinations of those two, with differing degrees of severity, or mixed aphasia

# Introducción

Varias condiciones de salud afectan nuestra habilidad de comunicación, trauma a la cabeza, tumores en el cerebro, patología en las cuerdas vocales, pérdida de la audición, e infarto cerebral (derrame). En este libro, nos enfocaremos en derrame cerebral, condición común en los Estados Unidos y en el mundo entero. Después de practicar Neurología por más de veinte y cinco años, he visto la frustración de familias cuando un derrame afecta a un miembro de la familia. Pacientes pierden la comunicación con sus queridos. Algunas veces, el paciente no puede expresarse y en otras, la familia no puede entender lo que expresa el enfermo. Esta incapacidad conduce a frustración y eventualmente depresión para el paciente. Para que familia, amigos, y personas que cuidan puedan entender cómo ayudar al paciente, hay que entender cómo el derrame afecta la comunicación. Las tres formas más comunes son:

- incapacidad de expresarse (afasia expresiva)
- incapacidad de comprender a otros (afasia receptiva)
- diferentes combinaciones y diferentes grados de severidad (afasia mixta)

# Introduction cont.

Speech pathologists can help patients regain communication skills to a significant degree. However, regardless of their exceptional efforts, a large number of patients remain unable to articulate their thoughts, especially those with expressive aphasia. Patients with receptive aphasia will have a harder time than those with expressive aphasia regaining understanding (Rowland 2005).

In the past, families created communication boards, learned sign language, or purchased expensive electronic devices to transmit information. Despite these efforts, sometimes the result was the unclear delivery of information, making it apparent that all these methods needed improvement and needed to become less complicated or expensive.

Even though American Sign Language (ASL) is a language in its own right, many signs require the use of two hands, an ability a patient with expressive aphasia may not have.

Furthermore, signing uses an imaginary rectangle in front of the body called the signing area (Flodin 2004), something that definitely requires modification for patients with hemianopia—a condition in which disturbances impair half of the vision in some patients (Ropper and Brown 2005).

# Introducción cont.

Patólogos del Habla ayudan a sus pacientes a recuperar toda comunicación posible. Pero, a pesar del esfuerzo y ayuda valiosa de los Patólogos del habla, hay un número significante de pacientes que no pueden recuperar la comunicación, especialmente los que sufren de afasia expresiva. Aquellos que muestran señas de afasia receptiva tienen más dificultad que los que sufren de afasia expresiva, en recuperar sentido de las oraciones (Rowland 2005).

En el pasado, en orden para mantener comunicación, familias creaban tablas de comunicación, aprendían lenguaje de señas, o compraban dispositivos electrónicos costosos. Desgraciadamente, a veces la comunicación permanecía confusa y/o dudosa. Los métodos anteriormente mencionados necesitan mejorar y ser menos complicados o costosos.

A pesar de que el lenguaje de señas es un lenguaje en sí mismo, muchos símbolos requieren el uso de dos manos, una habilidad que un paciente con afasia expresiva pudiera no tener.

Asimismo, algunos pacientes sufren de hemianopsia-característica adonde la mitad de la visión puede verse afectada, en estas personas las señas hay que usarlas en el área no afectada por la hemianopsia (Ropper and Brown 2005). Por lo tanto la creación de una forma de lenguaje más sencilla para ayudar a los pacientes con afasia expresiva se convirtió en una prioridad, y un estudio práctico se llevó a cabo.

7

# Introduction cont.

So creating another way to help patients with expressive aphasia became a priority, and a practical study evolved. ONE, a one-handed type of signing, was set in motion. This is not a new idea. It is based on ASL, but it became necessary to adapt some of its signs and create new ones. ONE is not intended to replace the work of speech pathologists but to help families communicate with the patient as soon as possible. Because stroke patients may develop paralysis on one side of the body, developing a one-handed sign language became imperative. It is not my intention to teach sign language to patients with expressive aphasia but to have a simple method of communication that uses some of the basic signs and some additional signs using only one hand. To continue with these ideas, I created a booklet that includes pictures, large text sizes, and written explanations to increase ease of use. Patients may even create their own personal signs, a motivation in the process of increasing communication.

After reviewing basic sign language books and the 400-year history behind sign language, I wrote this book for those who would like to increase their knowledge of signs (Flodin 2004). I have included a hand alphabet in the alphabet section.

# Introducción cont.

UNO, una forma de crear símbolos con una sola mano, se estableció. Esta no es una idea nueva y está basada en el lenguaje de señas, pero adaptaciones, creación de nuevas señas ha sido necesario. UNO no está diseñado para sustituir a los Patólogos del habla, sino ayudar a las familias a comunicarse con el paciente tan pronto como sea posible. Debido a que los pacientes con derrame (ictus) pueden desarrollar parálisis de un lado del cuerpo, el desarrollo de un lenguaje de señas con una sola mano fue imperativo.

No es mi intención enseñar el Lenguaje de Señas Americano (ASL) a los pacientes con afasia expresiva, sino que haya un método simple que utiliza algunas de las señas básicas y unas nuevas, con una sola mano. Por otra parte, el idioma de señas utiliza un rectángulo imaginario en el frente del cuerpo que se llama el área de señales (Flodin, 2004), definitivamente una modificación es necesaria para los pacientes con hemianopsia.

Para continuar con estas ideas, he creado un folleto que incluye dibujos, letras grandes, y explicaciones para aumentar la facilidad de uso. Los pacientes pueden incluso crear sus propias señas personales, una motivación en el proceso de aumentar la comunicación.

# Introduction cont.

As social creatures, we need to communicate. We unintentionally use our hands, our faces, and even our bodies when speaking. Giving patients an alternative form of communication during their time of healing helps them stay more motivated in the healing process and reduce angst and frustration.

# Introducción cont.

Después de estudiar libros básicos de lenguaje de señas, la historia de los 400 años anteriores, y para los que quieran aumentar su vocabulario de señas, he incluido un abecedario de mano en esa sección del libro.

Siendo el ser humano criatura social, necesitamos comunicarnos con otros seres. Sin querer usamos nuestras manos, cara, e incluso nuestros cuerpos al hablar. Dando a los pacientes una opción de comunicación diferente durante el tiempo de recuperación, les ayuda a estar más motivados en el proceso de curación, reduciendo angustia y frustración.

Dr. Roberto Mixco

# Explanations

- ➢ I assume people using this method do not know American Sign Language.
- ➢ When reading instructions, know that left and right hands are interchangeable.
- ➢ This method starts with some basics, such as finger spelling—the manual alphabet—and hand shapes recognized as being in the public domain.
- ➢ The amount of vocabulary is reduced; some signs have several meanings.
- ➢ It is important to use words in the correct context.
- ➢ Caretakers, family members, and friends can help teach the patient.
- ➢ The amount of vocabulary will be increased in the future.
- ➢ Suggestions and recommendations are welcome. Please e-mail them to oneuno1mixco@gmail.com. For further information an autor website is forthcoming.

# Aclaraciones

- Se asume que las personas aprendiendo UNO no tienen noción de Lenguaje por Señas.
- Cuando lean instrucciones, la mano derecha o la izquierda son intercambiables.
- Este método usa alfabeto manual y formas de la mano que son de dominio público. Estos se encuentran en libros básicos de Lenguaje de Señas.
- Como el vocabulario es reducido, muchos señas tienen varias interpretaciones.
- Usen palabras o señas con la interpretación adecuada dependiendo de la situación.
- La familia o amistades pueden ayudar al paciente aprender los signos o señas.
- Expansión del vocabulario se planea para el futuro.
- Sugerencias y recomendaciones son bienvenidas.
- Correo electrónico: oneuno1mixco@gmail.com. Para más información el autor tendrá un sitio web.

# Acknowledgments

This book is dedicated to all patients whose speech is affected by stroke. After experiencing my own patients' frustrations with communication, I decided to look for a way to help stroke victims. The idea of stroke patients using sign language is not new; however, I decided to create a simple, one-handed mode of communication for patients and their families. Clarification occasionally two hands are in a sign, but only one is active. This booklet contains clear photos and explanations.

Many people helped me develop and create this booklet. Immeasurable thanks to all who assisted in this development. Special thanks to Millie Sorger, former executive director of Island Health and Rehabilitation Center in Merritt Island, Florida, and Derek Ganary current administrator of the same center and to all the personnel in that institution who encouraged and welcomed this idea; my friend Brigit Kirchofer, her daughter Kirsten, and Betty Adkins, for their help with PowerPoint, computer technology, and my many other computer frustrations; Stephen Applegate, RN, and Sudy Shen for their encouragement and support; Susie Adams, RN, educator and previous manager of the neuroscience unit at Cape Canaveral Hospital and her staff, for their help with research; and Dr. Jonathan Charles for his technical support.

# Agradecimiento

Este libro está dedicado a todos los pacientes a los cuales su habla ha sido afectada por derrame al cerebro. Después de ver la frustración que un derrame cerebral produce en la comunicación de una persona, decidí encontrar una forma de ayudar a estos pacientes. El uso del Lenguaje por Señas no es una idea nueva, pero opté por crear un método de comunicación con una mano para pacientes y su familia. Aclaración, ocasionalmente dos manos aparecen en una seña, pero solo una mano esta activa. Este libreto contiene fotos y explicaciones.

Tengo que agradecer a muchas personas que ayudaron en una forma u otra a que este proyecto fuese realizado. Millie Sorger, ex directora ejecutiva de Island Health and Rehab Center en Merritt Island, Florida, y Derek Ganary administrador del mismo centro y a el personal de dicha institución que apoyó esta idea. Mi amiga Brigit Kirchofer, su hija Kirsten, y Betty Adkins por su ayuda con Power Point, computación, los efectos técnicos, y mis muchas frustraciones con tecnología. Stephen Applegate RN y Sudy Shen por su motivación y apoyo. Susie Adams RN , educadora y Ex Directora de la Unidad de Ciencia Neurológica en el hospital Cape Canaveral, y su personal por su ayuda con investigación de artículos relacionados. También al Dr. Jonathan Charles por su ayuda técnica.

15

# Acknowledgments cont.

Thanks to my friends and colleagues at Cape Canaveral and Wuesthoff hospitals who understood and welcomed this idea, my partner and colleague Dr. Miguel Rivera, and my office staff who backed up this effort; Meghan Adkins for her time, dedication, and grace in the modeling process; and Tammy and Mike for their direction in publishing.

And last, but not least, I am very grateful to my family: Anthony for encouraging me; Carlo for his abundant help with computer technology, including the late-night calls for instruction and my many computer frustrations; Giannina for not only modeling but also helping with my restricted computer skills; and my wife, Eva Marie, for her constant creative skills and imagination that led to the name of this booklet, her Photoshop skills, her editing skills in both languages, and her continued support.

Roberto

# Agradecimiento cont.

A mis amigos y colegas en los hospitales Cape Canaveral y Wuesthoff que tuvieron fe en mi idea y me empujaron a continuar. A mi socio y colega Dr. Miguel Rivera y a todo el personal de mi oficina por apoyar este proyecto. A Meghan Adkins por su tiempo, dedicación, y gracia en el proceso de modelaje. Tamara y Mike por su dirección en el proceso de publicación. Y finalmente, estoy agradecidísimo a mi familia. Anthony gracias por darme aliento y estimular mi imaginación. A Carlo, por su abundante ayuda tecnológica, por contestar mis llamadas de madrugada, y todas mis frustraciones con la computadora. A mi hija Giannina por su gracia en modelaje y por ayudarme tecnológicamente. Y a mi esposa Eva Marie, por su continua ayuda creativa que trajo a la creación del nombre UNO, a sus conocimientos de Photoshop, su habilidad editorial bilingüe, y por su inspiración continua, estoy muy agradecido.

Roberto

# Manual Alphabet—Finger Spelling  *Alfabeto Manual o Deletrear*

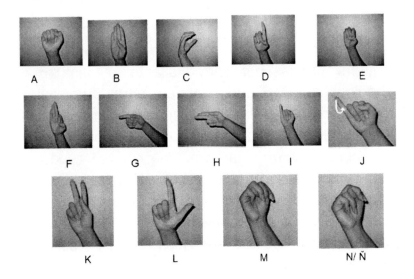

A      B      C      D      E

F      G      H      I      J

K      L      M      N/ Ñ

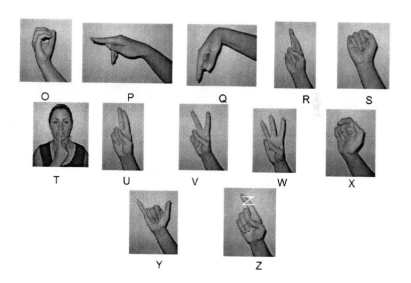

O      P      Q      R      S

T      U      V      W      X

Y      Z

# Basic Hand Shapes     *Formas básicas de mano*

Flat Hand    *Mano plana*

Clawed Hand    *Mano en garra, Zarpa*

Curved Hand    *Mano en curva*

Open Hand    *Mano abierta*

Closed Hand    *Mano cerrada*

Bent Hand    *Mano doblada*

# Interrogatives

# Palabras que Preguntan

| Interrogatives | Palabras que Preguntan |
|---|---|
| Who | Quien |
| Whom | Que |
| What | Cuando |
| When | Como |
| How | Donde |
| Where | Adonde |
| Which | Cual |

# Who, Whom, What, When, How, Where, Which

## Quien, Que, Cuando, Como, Donde, Adonde, Cual

Start with a flat hand, make a semicircle, and finish with the hand up and open.

*Comenzar con la mano plana después hacer un semi-círculo terminar con la mano abierta para arriba*

| Family and People | I, Me, He, Him, She, Her, You, It, Boy, Girl, Child, Children, Brother, Sister, Brother-in-Law, Dad, Father, Mom, Mother, Daughter, Son, Daughter-in-Law, Son-in-Law, Gentleman, Lady, Grandfather, Grandmother, Husband, Wife, Young man, Young Lady, Man, Woman | Familia y Gente | Yo, El, Ella, Tu, Usted, Esto, Niño, Niña, Niños, Hermano, Hermana, Cuñado, Papá, Padre, Mama, Madre, Hija, Hijo, Nuera, Yerno, Caballero, Dama, Abuelo, Abuela, Esposo, Esposa, El Joven, La Joven, Hombre, Mujer |

# I, Me   *Yo*

Point the right index finger toward yourself.

*Apunta con el dedo índice hacia ti.*

# He, Him  *El*

Move the right hand to the forehead as if gripping a hat and then point the index finger forward.

*Mover la mano derecha a la frente como tocando un sombrero. Después apuntar hacia adelante con el dedo índice.*

# She, Her  *Ella*

Place the thumb to the cheek, move it to the chin and then point the index finger forward.

*Con el pulgar de la mano tocar mejía, mover mano hacia barbilla. Después apuntar hacia adelante con el dedo índice.*

# You  *Tu, Usted*

Point at the addressee with the right index finger.

*Apuntar con el índice derecho a la persona en cuestión.*

# It  *Esto*

Point with the pinky
finger, placing the hand
near the waistline.

*Apuntar con el dedo
pequeño poniendo lo
sobre la cintura.*

# Boy, Girl, Child, Children

## Niño/a, Niños

Move the left hand up and down as shown.

*Mover mano izquierda de arriba a abajo.*

# Brother  *Hermano*

Put the hand to the forehead as though gripping a hat and then use the second and third fingers together, as explained in the picture.

*Mano hacia la frente como tocar un sombrero, luego usar el segundo y el tercer dedo juntos, como lo muestra la foto.*

# Sister    *Hermana*

With the thumb of the closed hand, go from ear to chin and then put the second and third fingers together, as explained in the picture.

*Con el pulgar de mano cerrada tocar desde el oído hasta el barbilla luego usar el segundo y tercer dedos juntos, como lo muestra la foto.*

# Brother-in-law / *Cuñado*

Put the hand to the forehead and then put the second and third fingers together and invert them (flip like a pancake).

*Mano a la frente luego invertir el segundo y tercer dedo juntos como darle vuelta a una tortilla.*

# Dad, Father / *Papa, Padre*

Put the right open
hand to the forehead.

*Mano derecha abierta
a la frente.*

# Mom, Mother / *Mama, Madre*

Put the right open hand to the chin.

*Mano abierta derecha tocando el mentón (barbilla).*

# Daughter  *Hija*

Put a hand to the cheek; move it to the chin and then to the heart with the hand flat.

*Mano hacia la mejía, luego hacia el mentón y luego al corazón con mano plana.*

# Son  *Hijo*

Put the left hand to the forehead as though gripping a hat and then close the hand to the heart.

*Mano izquierda a la frente como tocando un sombrero luego mano cerrada al corazón*

# Daughter-in-law / *Nuera*

Use the thumb of a closed hand to trace the cheek, move it to the heart, and then invert two fingers.

*Pulgar de la mano cerrada a la mejía, luego al corazón con mano abierta, y luego invertir dos dedos*

# Son-in-law / *Yerno*

Put the left hand to the forehead as though gripping a hat, move the closed hand to the heart, and then invert the second and third fingers together.

*Mano izquierda a la frente como tocando un sombrero luego con mano cerrada al corazón luego dos dedos juntos el segundo y el tercero invertidos.*

# Gentleman  *Caballero*

Touch the forehead as though gripping a hat and then touch the chest with the thumb, hand open.

*Mano a la frente como tocando sombrero, luego mano abierta y pulgar toca el pecho.*

# Lady  *Dama*

With the thumb of a closed hand, traces down the cheek. Then open the hand and touch the chest with the thumb.

*Pulgar de mano cerrada tocando mejía, mover mano hacia barbilla, y luego tocar el pecho con el pulgar, mano abierta.*

# Grandfather  *Abuelo*

Open hand to the forehead and then move it away.

*Empieza mano abierta a la frente y luego se aleja.*

# Grandmother  *Abuela*

Open hand to the chin
and then move it away.

*Mano derecha abierta a
la mejía luego se aleja.*

# Husband  *Esposo*

Put the hand to the forehead as though gripping a hat and then point to the ring finger of the other hand.

*Mano a la frente como tocando un sombrero luego señalar al dedo anular o de los anillos.*

# Wife  *Esposa*

Place the thumb of the closed left hand to the ear, move it to the chin, and then point to the ring finger.

*Pulgar izquierdo en mano cerrada desde el oído hacia el mentón luego apuntar al dedo anular.*

# Young Man / *El Joven*

Move the right hand to the forehead as though gripping a hat.

*Mover la mano derecha hacia la frente como tocando un sombrero.*

# Young Lady / *La Joven*

Use the thumb of the closed hand to trace the cheek down to the chin.

*Empezando con pulgar de mano, tocar la mejía, mover dedo hacia barbilla.*

# Man  *Hombre*

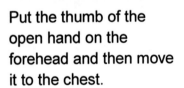

Put the thumb of the open hand on the forehead and then move it to the chest.

*Pulgar de mano abierta tocar frente luego pecho*

# Woman  Mujer

| Use the thumb of the open hand to touch the chin and then the chest. | *Pulgar con mano abierta tocar la barbilla luego el pecho.* |

# Feelings / *Sentimientos*

| | |
|---|---|
| Happy | *Contento, Feliz* |
| Upset | *Enojado, disgustado* |
| To Wish | *Querer* |

# Happy 😊 *Contento, Feliz*

The hand is open, except the third and fourth fingers, which are flexed.

*Mano abierta excepto el tercer y el cuarto dedos que están flexionados.*

# Upset, Angry  *Enojado*

Put a flat hand on the stomach and then turn the palm up.

*Mano plana en el estómago luego la palma hacia arriba.*

# To Wish, Want / *Querer*

With the left hand up and making the letter *C* and then moving down from the chest.

*Con la mano izquierda hacia arriba y haciendo la letra C, luego moverla hacia abajo desde el pecho.*

# Places / *Lugares*

| | |
|---|---|
| Bathroom, Toilet | *Cuarto de Baño, Inodoro* |
| Home | *Hogar* |
| Restaurant | *Restaurante* |
| This | *Esto, Este* |

# Bathroom,
# Restroom,
# Toilet

# *Baño,*
# *Excusado,*
# *Inodoro*

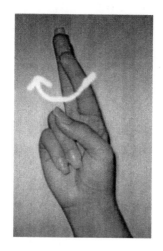

Draw the letter R with the hand and then twist it away from the body (as in the picture).

*Con la mano formar la letra R, luego gire la mano lejos del cuerpo (como en la foto).*

# Home 🏠 *Hogar*

Use the hand to draw the frame of a house in the air.

*Mano dibujando en el aire el marco de una casa.*

# Restaurant / *Restaurante*

Move the left index and middle fingers together from the right to the left part of the mouth.

*El índice y dedo medio izquierdos moviéndose de derecha a izquierda en la boca.*

# This / *Esto, Este*

Put the tip of the right index finger into the other hand.

*Poniendo la punta del dedo índice en la otra mano.*

| Modifiers (Adjectives): Quantity, Quality, Specificity | Modificadores (adjectivos): Cantidad, Cualidad, Especificidad |
| --- | --- |
| Bad | Malo |
| Big,Large | Grande, Largo |
| Busy, Fast | Ocupado, Rápido |
| Fine | Excelente |
| Good, Well | Bueno, Bien |
| Happy | Feliz, Contento |
| Mine | Mío, Propio |
| No | No |
| Other, Another | Otro, Otro Más |
| Same, Similar | Igual, Parecido |
| Slow | Despacio, Lento |
| Small, Little | Pequeño, Poquito |
| Yes | Sí |
| Upset | Enojado |

# Bad / *Malo*

Hand with thumb down, as shown in the picture.

*(Mano con el pulgar hacia abajo), como en la foto.*

# Big, Large / *Grande, Largo*

Make a big C with the
right hand.

*Mano derecha con la
letra C en grande.*

# Busy, Fast / *Ocupado, Rápido*

Snap the fingers.    *Sonar los dedos.*

# Fine, Good, Well /
# *Excelente, Bueno, Bien*

Turn the thumb up.    *Pulgar hacia arriba.*

# Mine / *Mío*

Pat the chest with a flat left hand several times.

*Poner la mano izquierda plana en el pecho varias veces.*

# No / *No*

This is a universal sign. It can be made in two ways:

- Either hand makes a stop sign.
- Finger shakes back and forth.

*Este signo es universal en dos formas:*

- *Puede poner la mano como deteniendo algo.*
- *El dedo índice oscilando.*

# Other, Another / *Otro, Otro Más*

Close the hand with the thumb up (as though making the letter *A*) and then turn it out.

*Mano, con el pulgar hacia arriba, (Mano en A) luego pulgar hacia afuera.*

# Same, Similar /
# *Igual, Parecido*

Put two fingers of the
right hand together.

*Mano derecha con dos
dedos juntos.*

# Slow / *Despacio*

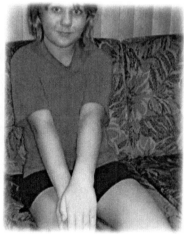

Put the left hand on top of the right hand, and move it slowly back and forth.

*Poner mano izquierda encima del brazo derecho y mover la mano hacia la otra, varias veces.*

# Small, Little /
## *Pequeño, Poquito*

Close the thumb and index finger.

*Pulgar y dedo índice cerca sin tocarse.*

# Yes / *Si*

Move the head up and down.

*Moviendo cabeza de arriba hacia abajo.*

# Actions          *Acciones*

| | |
|---|---|
| To Be | *Ser* |
| Able to | *Poder* |
| To Come | *Venir* |
| To Cry | *Llorar* |
| To Drink | *Beber, Tomar* |
| To Eat, Food, Meal | *Comer, Comida* |
| To Feel, Feeling | *Sentir, Sentimiento* |
| To Go, Go towards | *Ir, Ir hacia* |
| To Have, To Possess | *Tener, Poseer* |
| To Invent | *Inventar* |
| To Laugh | *Reír* |
| To Love | *Amar* |
| To Move, To Place | *Mover, Colocar* |
| To Raise | *Levantar* |
| To see, To Perceive | *Ver* |
| To Serve | *Servir* |
| To Share | *Compartir* |
| To Sign | *Hacer Señas* |
| To Sleep, To Doze | *Dormir* |
| To Smell | *Oler* |
| To Stop | *Parar* |
| To Taste | *Saborear* |
| To Think | *Pensar* |
| To Use | *Usar* |
| To Desire, To Want | *Desear, Querer* |

# To Be / *Ser*

Use clawed and then open hand.

*Mano en garra luego mano abierta.*

# Able To / *Poder*

Start with a closed hand and then move it toward the floor.

*Empezar con Mano cerrada luego mover en dirección del suelo.*

# To Come / *Venir*

Close hand faceup, flexing and extending all fingers.

*Mano cerrada hacia arriba cerrando y extendiendo los dedos.*

# To Cry / *Llorar*

Use the left index finger to point to the eye and then trace the cheek.

*Indice izquierdo apuntando al ojo luego deslizando a la mejía.*

# To Drink / *Beber, Tomar*

With the left hand in a *Y* shape, move it back and forth across the mouth.

*Mano izquierda en Y hacia la boca para atrás y adelante.*

# To Eat, Food, Meal /
## *Comer, Comida*

Move the hand to the
mouth a few times.

*Mano se mueve hacia la
boca varias veces.*

# To Feel, Feeling / *Sentir, Sentimiento*

Move the index finger up the chest with the other fingers extended.

*Mover el dedo índice en el pecho hacia arriba los otros dedos extendidos.*

# To Go, Go Toward / *Ir, Ir Hacia*

With the right index and little fingers pointing out, flex the other fingers.

*Indice y dedo pequeño derechos señalando hacia afuera.*

# To Have, To Possess /
## *Tener, Poseer*

Place the fingertips to the chest.

*Poner las puntas de los dedos contra el pecho.*

# To Invent / *Inventar*

Put the open left hand to the forehead and then move it forward.

*Mano izquierda abierta a la frente luego hacia adelante.*

# To Laugh / *Reir*

Move the left index finger
to the chin, move it toward
the ear, and smile.

*Mover índice izquierdo del
borde del mentón hacia el
oído.*

# To Love / *Amar*

Put the closed right hand on the heart (or chest).

*Mano derecha cerrada al Corazón o al pecho.*

# To Move, To Place / *Mover, Colocar*

Use a curved hand to indicate a surface and then move it.

*Mano en curva en una superficie y moverla.*

# To Raise / *Levantar*

Put your flat left hand in the up position and raise it.

*Poner la mano izquierda en posición plana y moverla hacia arriba.*

# To See, To Perceive / *Ver*

Put the left index and third fingers below the eyes in a Y shape and move them forward.

*Poner el índice y dedo medio izquierdos abajo de los ojos luego hacia adelante.*

# To Serve / *Servir*

Put the right hand
flat, palm up.

*Mano plana derecha en*
*posición hacia arriba.*

# To Share / *Compartir*

Put the left hand in the middle of the right hand.

*Poner mano izquierda en el medio de la otra mano.*

# To Sign / *Hacer Señas*

Make a circle with the hand.

*Hacer un círculo con la mano.*

# To Sleep, To Doze /
## *Dormir*

Use the flat right hand to touch one side of the face in a tilted position.

*Mano derecha en posición plana tocando un lado de la cara que esta inclinada.*

# To Smell / *Oler*

Use the flat right hand to touch the nose and mouth.

*Tocar nariz y boca con la mano derecha en posición plana*

# To Stop, To Wait / *Parar*

Put the right hand flat in front of you as in the picture—same as "no."

*Mano derecha en posición plana en frente como en la foto. Igual a no.*

# To Taste / *Saborear*

Put the index finger to the tongue.

*Poner dedo índice en la lengua.*

# To Think / *Pensar*

Put the right index finger in the temple area while flexing the other fingers.

*Poner índice de mano derecha en la parte temporal el resto de los dedos flexionados.*

# To Use / *Usar*

Put two right fingers together to draw a circle in front of you.

*Dedos índices y medio juntos haciendo un círculo.*

# To Desire, To Want / *Desear, Querer*

The right hand is curved with the palm facing up.

*Mano derecha en curva con la palma hacia arriba.*

# Things / *Cosas*

| | |
|---|---|
| Cup, Glass | *Copa, Taza Crystal, Vaso* |
| Paper | *Papel* |
| Water | *Agua* |

# Cup / *Copa Taza*

 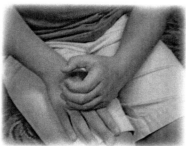

Put the left hand on top of the right hand to form a C.   *Mano izquierda encima de la otra en forma de C.*

# Glass / *Vaso, Crystal*

Touch the teeth with the left index finger.

*Indice derecho tocando los dientes.*

# Paper / *Papel*

Strike the base of the right hand with the left hand.

*Golpear con la base de la mano derecha en la izquierda.*

# References  *Referencias*

Atkinson, Dr. Joanna. 2002. "Deaf Stroke Project." (PDF documents.) Retrieved from http://www.dcal.ucl.ac.uk/team/joanna_atkinson.html.

BBC News. 2008. "Stroke Patients 'Need More Help.'" August 11. Retrieved from http://news.bbc.co.uk/2/hi/health/7422178.stm.

Damasio, Antonio, Ursulla Bellugi, Hanna Damasio, Howard Poizner, and John Van Gilder. 1986. "Sign Language Aphasia During Left-Hemispheric Amytal Injection. *Nature* 322, 363–365. doi:10.1038/322363a0.

Fant, L., and Barbara Bernstein. 2008. *American Sign Language Phrase Book.* New York: McGraw Hill.

Flodin, Mickey. 2004. *Signing Illustrated: The Complete Learning Guide.* New York: Penguin.

Gordon, Neil. 2004. "The Neurology of Sign Language." *Brain & Development* 26 (3): 146–150. doi:10.1016/S0387-7604(03)00128-1.

Rowland, Lewis P., ed. 2005. *Merritt's Neurology.* 11th ed. Philadelphia, PA: Lippincott Williams and Willkins.

Ropper, Allan, and Robert H. Brown. 2005. *Adams and Victor's Principles of Neurology.* 8th ed. New York: McGraw-Hill.

Schacker, Barbara Dean. 2005. "The Sensory Trigger Theory. Re-patterning the Brain for Speech After Stroke or Head Injury." Pathways. Retrieved from http://www.strokefamily.org/StrokeFamily/.

# References cont. *Referencias cont.*

Warner, Penny. 2001. *Learn to Sign the Fun Way.* New York: Three Rivers.

Whitely, Joan. 1998. "Sign Languages Can Improve Reading and Give Lift to Stroke Patients." *Las Vegas Review–Journal,* October 13. Retrieved from http://www.signit2.com/.

CPSIA information can be obtained at www.ICGtesting.com
Printed in the USA
BVOW05s2210190115

383971BV00001B/12/P